Touched by Love

LOVE AND DEVOTION (BOOK 4)

DONNA GODDARD

Also by Donna Goddard

Fiction

Waldmeer (Book 1 of Waldmeer)

Together (Book 2 of Waldmeer)

Circles of Separation (Book 3 of Waldmeer)

Faith (Book 4 of Waldmeer)

Pittown (Book 5 of Waldmeer)

Prana (Book 6 of Waldmeer)

Purnima (Book 7 of Waldmeer)

Nonfiction

The Love of Being Loving (Book 1 of Love and Devotion)

The Love of Devotion (Book 2 of Love and Devotion)

Love's Longing (Book 3 of Love and Devotion)

Touched by Love (Book 4 of Love and Devotion)

Dance: A Spiritual Affair (Book 1 of The Creative Spirit Series)

Writing: A Spiritual Voice (Book 2 of The Creative Spirit Series)

Strange Words: Poems and Prayers (Book 3 of The Creative Spirit Series)

Contents

Introduction

Touched by Love is about our body, relationships, and the spiritual path. It is vital to maintain, understand, and balance each of them. We must strengthen, expand, and extend all the energetic systems of our being. It takes work and commitment, but that is the purpose of life.

The **body** is the holder of our life force. Protect it, value it, and use it, but don't think it is an end in itself. We must work with every level of our being to make it more harmonious, efficient, and effective. Make a sacred space out of your body, mind, and spirit. Refine them every day with whatever practices work best for you. Don't ignore one aspect of your being out of laziness, ignorance, resentment or resistance.

The price of a successful **relationship** is devotion. Devotion is, essentially, commitment to something we value. What are we devoted to? Surely not what another person wants. I think most people would agree that being devoted to that would be problematic even with the best of people. So, what exactly are we devoted to? We are devoted to the wellbeing of another person. And we are devoted to the wellbeing of the relationship. We honour the value of the other person and we honour the worth of the relationship.

No one has to be a martyr on the **spiritual path**. On the contrary, everyone should be entirely selfish. Not selfish in the normal sense of the word, but selfish in the way of knowing that the spiritual path means we value everything that adds to our own well-being. When we love, we live with connectedness. When we forgive, we feel stress-free. When we create, we live with inspiration. When we follow our inner direction, we feel alive. Is that even a choice?

Love and Devotion Series

Love and Devotion is a four-book nonfiction series. To find the great Love, we must, one way or another, die the great death. Once that death is conquered, we won't have to die again. There is a grand and magnificent truth that radiates from within all of life and each of us. May you discover in your heart a sweet lightness, the luminescent glow of God's beauty, and a true appreciation for the wonderful gift of life which glows unmarred through every human error. We are loved by the Divine, loved into existence. That, in itself, is enough to reassure each one of us of our inestimable worth.

CHAPTER 1

Body

HOLDER OF OUR LIFE FORCE

PERFECT

My doctor didn't beckon me into her consulting room with her usual cheery greeting. Noted but unconcerned, I entered.

She paused for dramatic effect and said, "I suppose you could tell by my message that it isn't good news."

She looked at me to make sure that I was suitably attentive. The receptionist had phoned, a few days earlier, asking me to make an immediate appointment to discuss test results. I explained that I was interstate visiting family. I was told that a few days wait would be fine. Then I filed the issue in the back of my mind, and felt that all would be well.

A worried frown seemed the only appropriate response now. The doctor explained that I needed to have a skin area removed and that the specialist clinic would call me within a day. She added that I should tell my loved ones.

Confused and no longer sure how much of life and death was at stake, I said, "No, I'll tell them when everything is fine."

"You must tell them now," insisted the doctor.

I nodded but had no intention of doing so. I love my doctor. She's great, but she *is* a doctor.

A couple of days later, after reading the information from the Skin Clinic, I realised that the prognosis was much more optimistic than my doctor had inferred and the Clinic was confident that it could be handled successfully with day surgery. With renewed assurance that I would be around for the foreseeable future, I mentioned to my adult children that I had a small medical issue that needed to be sorted in the coming days. Done.

The day arrived. I was very nervous. Other than births, I've had very little medical intervention in my life, preferring to heal things in holistic ways, if at all possible. Anyway, I don't think anyone feels comfortable with the thought of being cut open for medical reasons even when we are grateful for the necessary intervention. Instinct tells us to protect our body. It is the precious and irreplaceable holder of the life-force which allows us the privilege of human existence.

The Clinic staff were professional and pleasant. All was going calmly. Until the intake nurse, that is. She seemed to find lots of mistakes on my long intake form which she resented having to fix. Then she took my blood pressure.

She turned to me with an accusatory glare and said, "Your blood pressure is *very* high." Pointing to my body, she added, "You are a little person. It should be much lower. You need to see your doctor as soon as possible to address this."

She waited for a response, so I mumbled, "Is it high? It's not normally, I don't think."

Suddenly, I felt that I had no idea what my blood pressure normally was. Maybe, I didn't know anything about my body. Maybe, I was reckless. Maybe, I had a serious heart issue as well as a skin issue. Maybe, my heart would kill me before anything else had a chance to. Panic was reigning supreme. I could feel my heart pumping wildly in my chest. If she had taken my blood pressure again, I'm sure it would have doubled.

Somehow, a small voice entered my racing brain, and I said to her, "I am nervous. Could that make it go up?"

She looked at me over her glasses and said, "You don't look nervous."

Feeling a spark of anger at her scare-monger tactics to vulnerable patients, I thought, *No, I don't **look** nervous. I'm trained not to look nervous. I'm trained to do terrifying Dancesport competitions and look as cool as a cucumber. And long before that, I was professionally trained to listen to people's problems and remain calm, helpful, and encouraging. No, I don't look nervous because I'm a mother and have had years of helping offspring with all manner of life's problems (even ones that make you want to cry to their face but, of course, you don't).*

Later, when I was settled into the operating room with several bright and positive medical professionals, I mentioned about the high blood pressure as I still wasn't sure if it actually was a problem.

The wonderful surgeon said with a hint of smile, "You are excited."

"I'm nervous," I explained.

She smiled more broadly and said, "Nonsense, you are just excited!"

We both laughed and thus the scene was set for a quick, successful, and painless procedure.

Before she did the incision, I must have had a panicked look on my face. One of the nurses asked kindly, "Are you okay?"

I took hold of her steady hand. She instantly responded by holding mine reassuringly and, for good measure, put her other hand on my arm.

I thought, *This is why it is much better to have caring, well-trained professionals in situations like this rather than loved ones. We don't want to worry family members, so we don't say if we need help. Anyway, the fear in their eyes exacerbates the problem.*

In fact, there is a tradition, in parts of India, that dying people go to a holy place to leave this life, rather than doing so in the presence of their family. Family ties can tend to drag out the leaving process and the transition becomes more laboured and complicated. Maybe, that's why many animals (like cats) prefer to go into isolation and hide (if they can) when they are unwell.

In the operating theatre, the nurses, other than the hand-holding one, took over the necessary jobs and my hand-holder turned into the resident entertainment. She was a natural-born story-teller.

Raised on a farm, along with her nine siblings, they had a great assortment of animals. At one stage, her father brought home a tiny, deserted baby animal. It was so young that they couldn't tell what it was. After bottle feeding it, they eventually discovered it was a fox. His favourite place to sleep was with the rottweiler. When the fox grew up, he made a den under the farmhouse. Every evening, he would trot off to hunt and, every morning, return to get a piece of "mother's best bacon" from Dad. One day, he didn't return. Apparently, Dad said that he had probably found a girlfriend. Later, my nurse friend realised that the local farmers were always shooting foxes and made the connection to her own loved foxy-family member.

This young woman had the wonderful story-telling capacity of vet and writer James Herriot of *All Creatures Great and Small* who wrote about his humorous, heartening animal adventures in country England around the 1930s. It's a gift.

Interrupting the stories which had only just begun, the surgeon said that all was finished and that she shouldn't need to see me again. Before they released me, one of the nurses retook my blood pressure. She pointed to the number on the machine and said, "See, it's perfect."

LIFE FORCE

The body is the holder of our life-force. Protect it, value it, and use it, but don't think it is an end in itself.

MORE FOREST

When you are worried, go to the forest. We, and our worries, get smaller as everything else gets more.

FOOD

Like everything else in life, we should eat consciously. We should learn to listen to our body about what to eat and how much – not too much, not too little, the foods which will not strain or poison our system. If the channel of communication is clear between our body and mind, it will tell us what we need for our body type, age, and level of activity while taking into account any health issues or changed circumstances which affect our metabolism. We can still treat ourselves with things we love, but we should do so in honest moderation and with awareness. Eating what is right for our individual system keeps our body healthy and active, and our mind awake and alert.

VEHICLE

If we would like a long and productive life, we must take special care of the vehicle God gave us to move around in while we are here. Abuse, neglect, and lack of maintenance will come back to repay us with pain, lethargy, dysfunction, and, of course, a shorter-than-possible lifespan. Further, from a spiritual perspective, it is difficult for us to pay attention to our consciousness-evolution if we are plagued with physical discomfort. When the body is comfortable and silent, we can more easily put our attention on higher pursuits.

TIME AND THE BODY

The more deeply attached we are to our physical body, the more problematic time will be for us. But if we hold our body loosely (like a well-selected, well-cared-for piece of clothing which is comfortable and suits us), we will find that time goes by easily and peacefully.

AGEING

Most people age way earlier than necessary. By thirty, many are old in themselves. By forty, most have lost the spark of life. By fifty, they are already senior. All of this is entirely preventable and, to a large extent, also reversible.

Ageing happens at all levels of our being, but the most obvious is the body. Use it or lose it. One of the reasons I dance, apart from my love of it, is that my teachers (who are generally younger than me) push me to keep using my body in ways that I otherwise might not. In large dance classes, I will often intentionally stand next to the twenty-year-old, very exuberant dancers as their energy (of which they have masses to spare) helps me. It is for this reason that very young children and very senior citizens go beautifully together. The elderly become ignited by the new life of children and the little children are calmed down by the loving, attentive energy of their senior friends.

Of course, you will be fighting a losing battle if you only

exercise your body and not your mind and spirit. When you use them all, they will gladly and efficiently work together. Although we cannot completely stop the march of time on our use-by-stamped bodies, we can have the blessings of a well-functioning and alive body, an active and bright mind, and a loving and expressive soul.

TOUCH THE EARTH

Touch the earth. Feel the sun. Listen to the passing wind. Let the healing power of nature restore your body. The very process of being alive means that we are constantly being inundated with fractious elements which work against our body's integrity. We need a healthy, quiet body to do whatever it is we have come to do. Touching the earth is one of the quickest, most effective ways of helping our body restore itself.

EXERCISE

Every day, we must exercise and use our body in a way that builds health, strength, longevity, and aliveness. The physical body is the foundation of our existence here. If it is not doing well, we will struggle to find the necessary resources to put into the other components of life. All the different levels of our being – physical, mental, emotional, and spiritual – should be fed, protected, nurtured, and cherished for the valuable way in which they serve us and facilitate our happiness.

CLAY

In yoga, or any physically demanding discipline (such as dancing), we turn our body back into clay so that it can be remade the way we want it. At the same time, if we wish, we can also remake our mental and ethereal bodies. The first *making* of ourselves (from birth) is generally very unconscious. The second one can be entirely awake.

BEING IN SYNC

If we are in sync with nature, we will be in sync with ourselves because, although we belong to Heaven, we are made from earth.

CLEANERS

Wind and water are God's cleaners. They are nature's healing agents for itself. Being made of earth, that includes us.

STOP TALKING

If you would like a simple practice which is 100% guaranteed to change you for the better - STOP TALKING. If that is too difficult, then cut your talking down by half. The idea is to become conscious of what we say and why. This practice (which I intuitively did at age 22 for some years) is transforming. Once you are aware of your talking, and it has lost all it's compulsiveness, then you will be free to talk as much as you want. You won't be so eager to talk, anymore.

STORY OF YOUR LIFE

Turn your life into a good story. Resolve to make the very most out of yourself.

INTIMACY

True intimacy is not a physical act but a state of non-resistance between two people.

BODIES TOUCHING

Travel inwards. Make yourself spectacular on the inside. Touch everyone with what is inside you. Bodies touching (although it has its place) is skin-deep. Minds touching is bigger. Souls touching is infinite.

IT WILL PASS

Mirko and Saleha were seventeen and each other's first love. On the cusp of youth and adulthood, they had a foot in both worlds. They fell in love with each other's being and then with each other's body. Perhaps, it happened at the same time. Saleha was a religious girl and had an ongoing battle with her ethics. Her normal response to Mirko's sexual advances was *no*. But Mirko was a young man. His body pushed for physicality and, besides, he was in love with Saleha. His persistence tended to win, one way or another.

They adored each other as young love does. They also fought. Young love has a million misperceptions about life. After all, it wasn't that long ago that *boys have boy germs* and *girls are useless creatures*. The two worlds converge and there is much to discover.

Mirko would later say that Saleha taught him to talk. Like many men, it is their female partner who will open the world of emotional connection, and demand that they participate. Mirko, in return, showed Saleha the power that women have over their men. To be loved as a pure thing is to feel the privilege of responsibility for another's happiness.

Saleha had only known one male body – his. At that age, other male bodies were not only disinteresting but somewhat alienating to her. Mirko's body, however, was both interesting and belonging to her. A woman can love her man and not want his body, however, to have both adds much weight to any

9

relationship. If one thing is not working, the other may be. Between the two, many rivers can be crossed without falling into the water and drifting hopelessly apart.

Long lasting sex appeal comes from inside us, not from outside. It moves outwards from our inner being. Self-possessed, present, protective men radiate a strong attractor field. Self-possessed, present, caring women also radiate a strong attractor field. Of course, we must work on all of the best qualities in both men and women. However, we also must be able to be the counterpart of our mate.

As much as Mirko loved Saleha, he, unlike her, had an eye for bodies other than that of his mate. He was a good-looking boy with a lot of sex appeal and it was all too easy to give in to readily available opportunities. Sex appeal and young manhood is a difficult combination to master. Mirko didn't try to master it. He didn't try at all. He went with the flow believing Saleha would not be hurt because she would never know. It took many heartaches, in years to come, for Mirko to learn that the gift of attractiveness must be used cautiously or its owner will become its slave. It is a sweet, seductive destroyer. For the duration of their relatively long, youthful relationship, Saleha knew nothing about Mirko's wanderings. That was something that only Mirko carried. He reaped the karma of shame.

Eventually, Saleha outgrew the relationship and knew that it was time for both of them to take a different path in life. It was a painful decision after the innocence and intensity of young love.

Some months later, Saleha heard from friends that Mirko could barely drag himself out of bed in the mornings after their split. He was grief-stricken. His parents were very worried about him. All sensible parents watch their offspring closely after relationship break-ups. The possibility of forever feeling utterly defeated and lost seems very real at that age.

Mirko's mother would coerce him out of bed, in the mornings, and send him off for the day. She blamed Saleha. Mirko was her oldest son. She was never going to like the girl that broke the mother-son spell. However, while a boy needs his mother, a man needs a lover.

Mirko's father watched him from a respectable distance. He told him occasionally, "Don't worry, son. It will pass. I promise you; it will pass. I promise you that you will feel better."

It was very appropriate, sensible, and loving advice for a first-time, love-lost victim of life's dramas. First love is deep and its demise is even deeper.

SACRED DANCE

Sufism is the mystic pathway of Islam. Its goal is union with the Divine. Part of its tradition is sacred dance in sacred places. The whirling dervishes twirl continuously with one hand pointed upwards towards the Divine and the other hand pointed downwards towards Earth. The dancing integrates body, mind, and spirit. It aims at elevating the dancer into a state of spiritual ecstasy. The mesmeric swirling of the Sufi dancers is a meditation. Anything which requires absolute attention becomes a meditation. Two hours in the dance studio, if you pay attention, is also a meditation. It naturally integrates the various aspects of oneself at different levels of being.

BURN

Some people have a poisonous impact on us. It is not necessarily in how they act towards us. That will be determined by social convention. It is the effect they have on our body and state of mind. It mostly comes from jealousy and competitiveness. Usually, we will instinctively know who is adversely affecting us. It's generally the first person or people who come to mind.

It's one thing to know this, but how do we get the poison out of our system? It's often wise to avoid certain people, but energy knows neither time nor space, so that won't fix the problem. We have to burn up the karma that is created by the other person. We burn up the accumulated content of the person in our system. Less appealing but equally important, we also have to burn up the accumulated content of ourselves. In this way, we are left with a clean, clear channel for the Divine to flow.

PATH INDICATOR

We should not be too quick to heal physical and mental discomfort in ourselves and others. The pain is trying to tell us something important about ourselves. If we find a way to delete the problem, without understanding its message, it will return, perhaps, in a worse form. It's better to patiently work with the problem until it dissolves in its own way. Thus, we will have benefited from the whole process. Be kind to yourself. Pain is not a judgement. It is a path indicator.

NATURE'S NATURE

The nature of nature is to heal and energise. Whenever we give it a little of our time and attention, it dissolves our problems, realigns our body, clears our mind, and awakens our spirit. And it's free. In return, we only need protect it, but we are simply protecting our own life-force and future.

NATURE'S EASE

We get fixated on various aspects of life insisting that they must work in certain ways. Inevitably, they don't. At least, they generally don't work in the particular ways that we have outlined. The great benefit of connecting with nature is that it doesn't insist on anything. Yet, it is highly functional. It is also intricately and immensely connected with a vast number of physical and energetic systems.

MOON-LOVE

Fall in love with the moon. You need its balance. Stay close to the sun. Walk every morning and take in its energy. We are only here because of it. Your soul belongs to the Divine, but your body belongs to the earth.

STILL POINT

Many people find that the easiest and quickest way to reach *the still point* is in nature. There is a tremendous amount of stillness in the busyness of nature. If we can find the still point in nature, we can find it in our own body. Our body is nature. The still point in nature is also the still point in us.

DAY AND NIGHT TRANSITIONS

If we train ourselves to be aware of the day/night transitions at dawn and dusk, our body will be more grounded and problem-free. The more stable we are as a body, the more freedom we will have to explore the subtler, finer dimensions of life without being adversely affected by them. Those other dimensions make us more receptive, empathic, creative, and joyous humans.

MORTALITY

The realisation of our mortality puts us on the spiritual path. Remembering it, keeps us there.

LIFE FRAGILITY

Once we understand the fragility of life, we live more consciously. We don't have enough time for fighting, hating, scheming, holding back, procrastinating, and numbing ourselves with any variety of tranquillisers. We want to use every day to better ourselves and the world we inhabit.

LIFE-LOAN

Death is not a possibility for the soul. However, the Earth vessel which the soul uses is most definitely on loan; to be given back completely at a specified time. While we have the loan, we should make the most of it. We should do what we sincerely are interested in, love fully, protect ourselves from those who wish us harm, and, ultimately, find the joy in the spectacular gift of this lifetime.

PLEASURE

If you are reading this, it means that you are alive! You have been given another day of life. Be grateful. If we do not take being here for granted, we will be more inclined to make the most of our time. We don't have to *do* more. We have to listen more – in the right way. Then our doing will not be a burden, but a pleasure.

WASTING YEARS

We generally don't like to be reminded that, sooner or later, we are going to die. However, having this thought in the back of our minds helps us to live well. My father's sudden death, when I was seventeen, certainly had a significant impact on my willingness to live life the way I sincerely wanted to. Otherwise, laziness, apathy, fear, indecision, and delusion can waste not only years but a whole lifetime.

THE SLY DECEIVER

Isobel watched Benedict walk unsteadily down his driveway towards the builders in the backyard. He hadn't dressed properly. He had no underwear on and his track pants were ripped so that anyone who looked (perhaps, it was impossible not to look) could see his backside. Somehow, it was still a good-looking backside for all that he had put his body through in recent years. There was no point telling him that he hadn't dressed properly. He was too sick. Along the way, things like dignity get lost.

The builders had been there for some weeks making a pool. Benedict wasn't short of money. It would have been better if he had been because the necessities of life would have pulled him back into some normality. The builders knew that Isobel was Benedict's ex-partner. Benedict repeated himself a lot. He reran stories incessantly in his head, and also out loud to anyone in his vicinity.

When Benedict stumbled back into the house, the head builder turned to Isobel and said, "I don't know why we are building this bloody pool. He's only going to fall into it, in a drunken stupor, and drown himself!"

Isobel said nothing. They all knew that the possibility of that happening was all too real.

15

A young apprentice lifted his head as Isobel headed for the house and said hopefully, "You've come to fix him up?"

He meant to sound light-hearted but the pity in his voice was obvious. Many people, even strangers, seemed to want to help Benedict. Isobel always found that very heart-warming. She didn't want to disillusion the young apprentice and so she smiled reassuringly and nodded as if that was what she had come to do.

She braced herself to enter the house. Any trace of smile left her face. It was worse than normal. Things were everywhere. The fridge door was left open. It was a pigsty. When she passed the bedroom, she was shocked to see that there was blood on the wall, a broken mirror on the ground, and a hole in the plaster. She couldn't remember seeing any new injury on Benedict. Perhaps, it was someone else's blood. That was even worse. It was pointless cleaning any of it up. She had done that many times. This time, it was just too dreadful.

After a while, Benedict slumped onto the lounge and said, with head in hands, "I know I need help."

Isobel had heard it before, but he still wouldn't go to rehab. The terrible thing about rehab is not so much the physical withdrawal from the alcohol or drug. That is its own special kind of drama. The real terror is what is inside the person without any sedation: the pain, longing, hopelessness, memories, anger, and fear. Isobel washed a mug, made Benedict a cup of tea, and left. What else could she do? He wasn't a minor. He wasn't mentally ill. He wasn't sick enough for a hospital. He wasn't dead. Yet. It was his right, as an adult, to destroy himself. She left the house, but he was never far from her thoughts.

Alcohol and drugs are the sly deceivers, thought Isobel, *floating in, like a party, and then way outstaying their welcome. The longer they stay, the less their hosts can see them.*

For many people, they become a dependence. The dependent always says that it has no adverse effect on them. Every medication has a side effect. Alcohol and drugs are the most readily available, socially-supported, popular-choice medication there is.

Recalling a quote that she read recently, Isobel thought,

Man cannot really live without attachments, but mostly we are reaching for the wrong attachment.

— THOMAS HORA

For some people, like Benedict, alcohol and drugs become a full-on addiction. Their deadly hold then becomes a very serious fight for survival. They will take everything. No mercy.

Isobel wanted to shout out to the world, *Get out of here you foul destroyer. I see what you are doing.*

However, she couldn't because the rest of the world had already embraced them like a trusted friend. To her, the thought of putting a poisonous substance into one's body with the intention of losing one's normal state of awareness seemed very foreign.

Why waste your precious life or even a precious day? she thought.

A few weeks later, Benedict changed his mind (what was left of it) and went to rehab. It was the first of many stays. The battle was far from over, but the time it took for him to start drinking after rehab visits became longer, and the time it took for him to decide to go back to rehab, after relapses, became shorter. He was not in the death zone for quite so long. He was very slowly getting better.

One day, Benedict said to Isobel, with tears in his eyes, "I'm so sorry. I'm so sorry for all of it."

Isobel didn't bother to hide the relief in her voice, "The only thing that matters is that you are getting better now."

Benedict continued, "There are whole periods of time that I cannot even remember."

Isobel smiled as if it was of no consequence, but thought, *It's probably just as well!*

I Was There

I walked with you,
I never left.
You thought I did,
but I did not.

Every step of the way,
every glass you held,
every spirit you took,
every thing you killed.

Right there with you,
watching it all.
Every stupid, destructive
heart-wrenching thing.

Still alive.
God only knows how.
Still alive.
I saw it all.

No, I wasn't gone,
I felt it too.
Knew every fear,
knew the despair.

Every bruise,
every cut,
every cry,
every damn bit.

Right there,
right there.
Never gone,
always there.

There was another who
watched as well.
The boy you loved,
he saw it too.

Said little, as he
knew not how
to talk of things so
brutal and raw.

You engraved him
on your wrist,
on your pulse,
so your heart

could recall
why it beat,
why to live,
not to die,
why to try.

PHYSICAL MATTERS

Physical distance matters for physical matters. However, even physical life is not as physical as it seems as the vast majority of it is the space in between the solid. Likewise, the vast majority of what matters most in life is the stuff in between the physical - the breadth of ideas, the depth of emotional connection, the height of spiritual inspiration. All of that requires neither space nor time. For the greater part of life, we are free.

CERTAIN DEATH

Only those who have crossed paths with death ponder the meaning of life. From the moment we are born, our passing is assured. Everything else in life is subject to change. But this one thing is certain. We shall, one day, leave. Only when we understand our mortal nature, do we live fully and love fearlessly. We throw ourselves into life because we are here but for a moment.

BRIEF TIME

If we remind ourselves that we are here for a brief time, our choices, while here, will become much more meaningful, appropriate to our individuality, and satisfying. We don't have to be told to stay in contact with the Divine when we know we need assistance to make this life count.

CHAPTER 2

Relationships

WHAT WE VALUE

DEVOTION

All significant relationships have a price. It's not that relationships are a sacrifice. After all, who wants a life of sacrifice? It is more a matter of priorities. We can't do everything in life and we can't be with everyone in life. In choosing what we will do and with whom, we automatically make priorities. If something is at the top of our list then other things have to come second or third or last.

The price of a successful relationship is devotion. Devotion is, essentially, commitment to something we value. What are we devoted to? Surely not what another person wants. I think most people would agree that being devoted to that would be problematic even with the best of people. So, what exactly are we devoted to? We are devoted to the wellbeing of another person. And we are devoted to the wellbeing of the relationship. We honour the value of the other person and we honour the worth of the relationship.

We make the decision that someone else's life is as important to us as our own. This is necessary because there are endless things in life which will pull us in different directions and will work against the stability of the relationship. No relationship survives or, more accurately, survives happily without a joint commitment to the genuine happiness of the other person. We do not have to sacrifice our destiny, talents, friendships, or ambitions but their impact on the other person has to be seriously considered.

When times are uncomfortable, challenging, not what we wanted/imagined, or actively distressing then we should not revert to dishonesty, nondisclosure, or manipulation to get our own way. What good is getting our own way if that way is destructive to our partner? We will end up suffering, anyway, from the painful demise of our relationship. A different, new, reformed way can always evolve. Some things aren't that important and disagreement is of minimal importance. Some things have a huge impact on the life of both people and some sort of agreement has to be earnestly sought. Compromise is not difficult when the people involved care about the emotional, mental, and physical health of the other.

Although it seems too obvious to say, there has to be a commitment to doing no harm in the life of the other person. Many people, consciously or unconsciously, view relationships as a type of business partnership where we try to get the most that we can for the least price. That is not even a good business relationship.

The health of a relationship is dependent on daily attention. I remember listening to a radio conversation with an exasperated wife who was complaining that her husband did not tell her that he loved her.

"When we got married," said the equally frustrated husband, "I told you that I loved you. That stands unchanged until and if such time I tell you that I don't love you!"

In his mind, it was black and white. He was committed to the marriage. It was not necessary to keep reaffirming that.

Understandably, his answer was not received well by a wife who needed more emotional intimacy.

Like a garden, our relationship needs consistent attention if we want it to remain alive, vibrant, and flourishing. If we forget about our garden for long stretches of time, we will find that something other than what we designed will have taken over the garden beds. The garden beds will become full of weeds. The weeds will start choking the plants. Maybe, some new plants will start growing from seeds which have blown into the garden, taken root, and claimed the garden for itself. They might even be great looking plants but they will not be the ones we intended for our garden. If we love our garden, we will want to watch over, protect, feed, and water it.

As much as we may love and enjoy someone (or, at least, for a reasonable amount of the time), relationships are primarily a responsibility. Often, people talk about the joy of a new baby as something wonderful given to the parents as if the child is for their pleasure. Of course, children are a gift. However, in looking at my three newborns, I never had the feeling that they were, even remotely, here for my benefit. On the contrary, I looked at each one and felt the great responsibility of a tiny, totally dependent human. It was my task to keep their little bodies safe and also their minds and souls. In general life, I was acutely aware of the effect of everything negative on the forming consciousness of children. I frequently looked at parents and thought, *Do they not realise the effect that their words and actions have on their child?* Yes, indeed, it seemed to me an almighty responsibility.

If we don't want the responsibility of another life (tiny or adult) then it is better to abstain from the commitment. Otherwise, we will end up hurting the other person, ourselves, and numerous other people along the way. Falling in love is relatively easy. All we need is an open heart, the ability to see good in others, and a willingness to engage intimately with another's heart. Falling in love versus committed love are as different from each other as feeling that a baby is here for our own benefit versus embarking on the long, conscientious responsibility of raising a beautiful, well-adjusted human. A partner is not a newborn (thank God) and we can expect a great deal more reciprocity. Nevertheless, the commitment to hold another's life as being as important as our own is the same.

RESPONSIVENESS

When we love someone (or everyone), we don't think about what we do or don't want to do in response to their needs. If there is a need, we respond. We are responsive because we care.

BREATHING CREATURES

Relationships are living, breathing creatures with a life force of their own. They cannot be stuffed in a cupboard or placed on a mantelpiece. They are not an assumed right. They need to be tended with care. They need daily attention. Not forgotten, but neither spoiled. No doubt, they are time consuming, but it is the attentive, respectful, caring, humorous time together which feeds them. Without that, the person may still be there, but the relationship won't be.

ARGUE WELL

A couple that can argue well can also live together well. This does not mean that arguing is valued in and of itself. However, conflict is inevitable when two different people try to share their lives at many different levels. It is very important that neither is scared to speak up. It is vital that each can honestly say how they feel and what they think. Each must know that they are respected, even if disagreed with. Only in this way, can a genuine, open, and deep bond be grown between the two.

FORCE

Don't FORCE things.

1. Don't force people. Inspire them, encourage them, help them, but let them move under their own steam.
2. Don't force situations. Work with them, contribute to them, do your best, but you don't know everything. Things need to evolve in their own way.
3. Don't force yourself (in body, mind, or spirit). Pay attention, be committed to your own well-being, make the most of your life, but you are part of the universe. Your life is not your sole making.

LOVE

When we love another person, it is we who love. The other may ignite our love but it is we who decide to love. We need to magnify our decision to love whether people love us or not.

HONESTY AND NEED

We make alliances and relationships in life because of our needs: physical, emotional, social, financial, professional and spiritual. We don't make them because of other people's needs. If we are honest about this then we will be grateful for what-ever needs are being met. We will not blame people if they are not able to or not willing to fulfil other needs. The unstated but fundamental basis of the arrangement is clear, at least, to us. Only when we understand our motives are we capable of forming life in a way that is beneficial to us and others. Honesty is power in terms of personal development.

APPROPRIATE RELATIONSHIPS

We need to distinguish between love and relationships. As spiritual students, we learn to love everyone. However, we have different types of relationships in our life, and we act accordingly. This is relatively easy to do once we realise that our ability to love has nothing to do with other people. It has everything to do with our state of mind. That is what we work on - our own consciousness. Every day, we try to become more loving within our own being.

CONSCIOUS USE

Looking at social media can ignite a feeling of inadequacy in people; that everyone is more gorgeous, has happier relationships, many more friends, more accomplished careers, more talented children, and all round more fantastic lives. In reality, the average person is fortunate to have a fleeting few of these things. People believe others would ridicule them if they knew what they were really like, and so most people pretend. Pretension always breeds duplicity. It means we will say and act one way but, in a million other ways, we will convey a different message.

I remember looking at the social media page of a person I knew well. It was full of adoration for his wife and children. They were a gorgeous looking family. It was most impressive. However, I knew that the man had ambivalent feelings about his wife and had an eye for love interests outside the family. So, to me, the whole thing seemed silly, although common enough. He did not mean to hurt anyone or intentionally deceive, although he did both. Like most people, he was struggling to find his happiness. It would have seemed like the best available option to him. Isn't this typical of human nature, in one form or another?

Social media is a mirror of human nature – no worse, no better. Some people divorce it in order to get rid of one such problem. One could also choose to use it consciously. If we talk consciously in face-to-face life, we'll use social media consciously. That's all social media is - talking. People use it exactly the same way that they normally converse: superficial or deep, depressing or jollying, fear-mongering or sensible, divisive or healing, blabbing or watching, never shutting up or never stops contributing, making fun of others or having fun with life, always wanting something or always giving something, sneaking or accounted for, self-oriented or all-oriented.

TRUST

If you want to know who you can really trust, think of who is willing to tell you things about yourself that you don't want to hear. Think of who is willing to tell you such things, but who loves you still. Their love for you is more than their need for you to like them.

ATTRACTIVENESS

The most attractive thing in the universe is to care.

FALLING IN LOVE

You have to fall in love. Falling in love makes you malleable. It makes you new. You get fresh eyes. Growth is inevitable. Those who fall in love with nothing, change nothing. Ignorance and arrogance are unfortunate, but common, bedmates. Falling in love dissolves the arrogance. Something becomes more important than our own mind. Ignorance will be on the back foot and change gets a foot in the door.

THE TROUBLE WITH FALLING IN LOVE

Although highly enjoyable (at certain stages), falling in love is problematic. The first problem is *who* we can fall in love with. We can fall in love with anyone. A gay person when we are not gay (or maybe we are gay but the wrong gender). A married person who happens to be not married to us (or we could be the married person falling in love with someone other than our partner). An unsuitable person in terms of age, personality, lifestyle, or future goals. Or, worst of all, a person who doesn't love us in return.

However, even if we fall in love with a gender-appropriate, sexual-orientation-appropriate, availability-appropriate, age-appropriate, life-goals-appropriate person then falling in love is still highly problematic because of the inherent dynamic of the process itself.

This leads to our second problem – the design of the falling in love mechanism. The mechanism of falling in love is designed to gain a thing which it is incapable of gaining. It seeks wholeness but inevitably leads to pain, fear, and failure. We need not give up on love, but we do need to understand it.

The nature of human consciousness is to seek completeness. It's a good intention, but the nature of human consciousness is also to look for it in the wrong places. We have an instinctive drive which seeks wholeness in every way. At the physical level, it is perceived as joining with another, preferably, loved and desired body. Regardless of the shallow talk and jokes that people commonly exchange about sex, most people truly look for a deeper sense of connection and unity in their sexual relationships.

Need I tell you about the innumerable problems people have in this pursuit? If the body is fragmented and in need of another body to complete itself, the emotional body is even more fractured. The success of the venture to find emotional completeness is about as successful as the physical one. How can we approach the whole arena of love with a different understanding and thus a different outcome?

On a practical note, time helps with many things. It helps with infatuations that are going nowhere. Before long, bits of reality dismantle minor crushes and attractions. If it is a major but unconsummated falling in love, it may take a few years, but even an intense emotional attraction will generally succumb to the intrusions of life. For example, if one falls in love with a person who is involved with someone else and, after a few years, that person is still in the same relationship then even the most romantic person will generally accept their losses and move on. Sometimes, the so-called loved one has turned into a God in the mind of the in-love one who has attached their emotional barrenness to that person. The real person and the one in the mind of the love-stricken person become totally unrelated. Usually, however, time will bring about the dissolution of infatuations that go nowhere.

Not only does time dissolve infatuations that go nowhere, it also dissolves relationships once they are established. After a few good years, the stuff of life, the brokenness of people, the dissatisfaction people feel with what their mate was supposed to be, and the inability of couples to live harmoniously becomes painful enough that many couples break up at this point. Alternatively, they may stay together but live out the rest of their relationship in secret despair or outright rage. If all of this sounds rather depressing then we are ready to understand what makes love really work. Is there an alternative to abandoning relationships, secret despair, and the stress of conflict? Yes, indeed, there is, but it has little to do with falling in love and much to do with the development of true love.

Truly loving people are uncommon. They are as uncommon as awake people. Our success in learning about love will directly correlate to our level of happiness. It is certainly worth persevering with the learning process which involves a great deal of honesty, introspection, and forgiveness. Even if we are the only one in the relationship on that path, it doesn't matter. We will still be blessed with our own happiness and isn't that the bottom line of what we all want? Our first responsibility is to create a happy life for ourselves. If the other person in the relationship learns to also value love, honesty, and forgiveness then the relationship will transform, usually slowly, into a strong connection which is good for the couple and others alike.

Even though true love is very different to falling in love, we mustn't stop the fall of falling in love. There's a certain surrender to falling in love. We have to let go of something of ourselves to fall in love with another person. When it becomes clear that love is not maintainable under the same belief system that made us fall in love, we can reassess our course. After the fall of falling in love, there is a steep climb back up again but we can make sure that we are climbing in the right direction. And that makes all the difference.

FAMILY

Our family is a place where we can have a profound impact on other people. Try to make that impact as positive, life-enhancing, and encouraging as possible.

FAMILY SAFETY

Make a circle around you where there, at least, you do not have to put energy into protecting yourself as you have to in the world. Hopefully, our families are this for us. And also, our most trusted friends. And, if fortunate, even our work environments.

INCLUSIVITY

Self-oriented people are inclusive only of those they believe will further their own motives and causes. More evolved people understand that inclusivity is the most productive and positive way to be. As such, their endeavours are life-enhancing, successful, and significantly contributory. Truly inclusive people do not gossip, listen to gossip, seek to pull other people down, view competition as a play of personal power, or try to gain benefit from someone else's suffering. Instead, their eyes, mind, and talents are directed towards whatever is best for everyone in any given situation.

BURNING UP

When we look at people, or think of them, we should try to recall the best we have seen in them, and delete all that is below that. Every evening, before we go to sleep, we should recall the events of the day which hurt or worried us and picture them as being burned up in the fire of compassion and Divine light. This process relieves us of having to carry the weight of other people's problems. If we are a serious student of life, we will not only burn up the day's bad, but we will burn up the day's everything, so that the next morning is a new, fresh, clean slate of possibility.

TREAD WITH CARE

That which holds us together is delicate. Tread with care. Take nothing for granted. Respect what others give you, but don't give what you shouldn't. Start the day with appreciation that you have it.

COMPASSION

One morning, in a coffee shop, the manager growled several derogatory and unwarranted demands at the staff member standing next to her. The staff member was a young, inexperienced girl. She looked defeated. She had probably had too many similar remarks thrown her way that day.

To protect the girl, I wanted to say to the manager, *You are being mean.*

I opened my mouth and said, "You are…"

But then I stopped. I saw in the manager's eyes frustration and anxiety.

I changed my tone and continued quietly, "You are… very stressed."

The manager's look softened and she started to laugh. I laughed too and then others around us joined in.

"I have had a bad morning," said the manager.

Her whole demeanour changed. She was grateful that she felt better. Before I left, she came up to me and offered me a free coffee card.

"Your coffee was late," she said by way of explanation.

My coffee wasn't late. The timely idea of a compassionate response, instead of a reactive one, made everything right on cue.

GIVE IT UP

When I started working with Thomas Hora (as a spiritual student), he was very big on forgiveness. I was only twenty-two-years-old but already there seemed so much to forgive. We only accumulate more and more over the years. So, it's very important to learn what to do with the hurt we collect. True forgiveness is not sacrificing ourselves to someone else's nasty, destructive ways. It's something much more effective than that.

The simplest way to define forgiveness is to give up blaming.

— THOMAS HORA

CLEAN IT UP

It is highly beneficial to put aside set periods for cleansing and healing processes. You will be amazed at how much stuff you actually carry around with you. If you would like to be healthy, vital, clear-minded, and good-willed such practices are essential. Forgiveness will always be a vital element of our inner work because most of what we are doing is burning up karma - our own and other peoples.

WHO?

No person or partnership is worth betraying ourselves. If we choose a person or partnership over our true Self, little by little, we will die inside anyway. If we choose our own truth, without fear or anger and with love for all, we will save ourselves and also others along the way. *Who* we save is not our choice. It is theirs.

JEALOUSY

We underestimate the destructive nature of jealousy and how it goes from bad to worse. As each conniving step is taken and fails, it only gets sicker. One day, in despair, it may realise that all was for naught. The cherished thing was not only never going to be attained, but it also could never do what was hoped for.

ENEMIES AND FRIENDS

An important aspect of the spiritual path is to understand the nature of other people's jealousy. Unfortunately, jealousy is rife amongst normal people. The happier and more successful we are, the more we will have to deal with it. Do not underestimate the powerful and negative impact that jealousy can have on your well-being and life. It can come from people you know, people you don't, enemies, and also friends. Fortunately, once seen, its power is significantly reduced, and with the conscious use of our spiritual practices it can be effectively disarmed.

POWER

Only love has power – to heal, to release, to forgive, to protect, and to make life happy.

TO BE LOVED

Everyone wants love. Not necessarily to be loving - that involves the work of transformation! But, to be loved. Most everyone feels that if they were loved (and, in particular, loved by specific people), then they would be happy. Wrong. Firstly, most people aren't such great lovers. Secondly, that approach doesn't work. We have to start with life's inevitable pain. Then, we need to look for a way to live that actually works.

ANOTHER CHANCE

It was Daniel and Bethany's time. It was a gift from life or, perhaps, it was life's little joke to itself. Dan and Beth were not laughing. It was too important and promising.

It did not take long for Dan to turn to Beth, one day, and say, "If I asked you to marry me, would you say yes?"

Beth was surprised; such a serious question. Daniel's eyes would not let hers turn away. They were tunnelling with the demand, *Answer me, now.*

Before her mind could manage to push forth some reasonable concerns, even objections, a smile jumped into the arena and smoothed itself over Beth's mouth. The deal was sealed in the passing of a few seconds. For the shortest breathing space, Dan and Beth relaxed. The moment was so piercingly innocent that both felt naked and embarrassed. Perhaps, too much of themselves had been shown to the other. It was a marriage proposal that would go horribly wrong.

In retrospect, the signs were clear, but Beth didn't want to believe them. The coming months grew more and more confusing until she could not remember if Dan even vaguely liked her. One final day, he casually announced to her, as if it was of little relevance, that he had been lately meeting up with an old friend. They had reignited their friendship and he was going to move to her city, start a relationship, and live with her. Beth was incredulous.

The sorrow would have been debilitating except that Daniel, in his guilt, had decided that the best approach was to act like there was no reason why Beth would be anything but happy for his new adventure. This brought the fire out in Bethany.

How dare he hurt me like that, she fumed to herself. *How dare he ask for my love and trust, and then disregard it as if it never happened.*

Dan was much bigger than Beth and he was a man not challenged lightly. She hit him, and didn't hold back. It was not the first time Beth had hit Dan. He hated it intensely because he could not hit her back. He seethed with fury. They both stared at each other like the world was about to explode. At least, it was an even match. Seeing that Dan meant to carry through with his plan, and to do so with no remorse, Beth threw herself towards the door with disgust that knew no bounds.

After a while, the anger faded but something worse took its place – grief. Every morning, following on the heels of waking consciousness, Beth would hear the words, *It's over. Accept it.* A thousand times, she scolded herself, *Why did you give him your heart? You knew it was a dreadful idea.* But she did give him her heart. It was already done. Once the contract is signed, it can only be nullified by a painful untangling.

Beth wondered how Dan was going in his new relationship. She felt that he must have adjusted by now. He must be happy. It was his decision, after all. Every day, she would release him in her soul. *How many times must one release the same person* she wondered.

Sometimes, Beth would dream of a friend from another land. The friend had many disguises, however, she always recognised the friend by the way they talked, the advice they gave, and the energy field they left behind.

"If you didn't give Daniel your heart," said the Friend, "he could not heal. It's the price you paid for his healing."

Beth wondered if the price was worth it. Maybe, it was all for naught anyway.

"Will I see him again?" asked Beth.

"Yes, you will see him," replied the Friend. "He never went

to live with the girl. He didn't even start the relationship. There was no need of it once you left. He didn't love her, but he needed a reason to make you leave. If one cannot trust that one will be loved even at one's worst, the healing cannot begin. One will always be lying about what is inside oneself."

"Will he heal?" asked Bethany.

"That, my dear Bethany, is the enthralling story of life," said the Friend. "It is written by the most brilliant of writers, you know. For now, it is enough for you to know that love is its own reward."

* * *

Five years later, Bethany was looking at the rundown cottage. It was perfect. For some reason, Dan seemed to think otherwise as he looked suspiciously at the wildly creaking floorboards. Beth was too busy to notice as she gazed with mounting excitement at the ceiling with an array of house spiders and other insects happily living their communal life.

Dan glanced sideways at the real estate agent of the quiet village as if to say, *Why in God's name did you bring us here? It's a disaster.*

The real estate agent couldn't help but have an apologetic look on his face. He was of the same ilk as Dan.

When Bethany was a child, her family would often set out on the five-hour drive to their relative's farm. It was a long drive for a little girl. Although she never mentioned it to anyone, she had a game that she played. Bethany knew the houses, on the way, well. Her favourites were the rundown ones with rusty roofs, tall grass, and broken fences. For each forgotten cottage, she dreamed about how she would fix it up. She imagined living there and, every day, making a little progress with the restoration of her charge. She thought about the sweeping, painting, rubbish removal, and gardening. She knew that given a chance, her charges would turn into beautiful, loving, and loved homes. She never told anyone her game because no-one ever told her to do it. It was an idea from the ether and it seemed best that it remained there.

Bethany turned brightly to Dan and held his arm, "Can you feel it? It's wonderful."

"No Beth," he said emphatically. "I can't feel anything except disgust. The plaster is falling off the walls. The roof is leaking. God only knows how much asbestos is lying around the house. There are rat droppings everywhere. The garden is full of rubbish. I hate it." To make sure Bethany had no doubt in her mind of his position on the matter, he stared into her eyes and repeated firmly, "Bethany, no. It's horrible. Let's go."

Ben walked out the door in disgust. The agent looked awkward and followed Ben sympathetically.

Bethany glanced through the dirty, broken window and spotted a rose flowering beneath an overgrown mass of blackberry bushes. A little bird bobbed its head and seemed to say,

This garden has life. It has just been forgotten for a long time. You are the one.

Unfortunately, Dan didn't want to be any part of that one. And so, the search went on for the perfect house.

Dan tried being conciliatory and said, "Come on, Beth. That house is only fit for the bulldozer. Let's look at all the other houses that the agent has lined up for us. We will find some other place that you will love even more."

It was a very sensible suggestion, if only Beth could bring herself to believe it. They spent the afternoon driving around. As they pulled up outside the houses, she made a conscientious effort not to look completely disinterested. Bethany felt that the original cottage was the most beautiful in the village. She almost felt sorry for the other residents of the town.

However, there was no need for pity because no-one else seemed to think the same way. Mostly, they preferred their own large and fabulous houses.

After some months, the rundown cottage was so cheap and everything else was so expensive that Dan took a deep breath, wondered why he was agreeing, and they bought the little house.

As much as Dan resented the broken and fragile state of the cottage, he also secretly hoped that it could be saved. Soon, it became one of the loveliest cottages in the village. Although it wasn't an instant love affair for Dan, he grew to love it. He felt happy and relaxed there. Every little improvement, somehow, reassured him that healing is not only possible but inevitable.

As for Bethany, she loved it from when she was a young child looking out the window of their family car, watching the passing paddocks dotted with the neglected homes that needed another chance.

RESPONSIBILITY

Whenever we are upset about anyone or any situation, it helps to start from the premise that it is what it is. People are what they are, at any given level of their understanding, and will act accordingly. Once accepted, we can take daily responsibility for doing OUR best with our own unique qualities and capabilities. We are responsible for our own effort, not the outcome. Be assured – the outcome of any genuinely good effort, one way or another, is simply a matter of time. Life is always trying to align with its highest expression.

DETRACTORS

When we keep our eyes on what we want to achieve in life, we pay little attention to those who cannot.

PLAY FAIR

We can ask for things to be fair without imposing one ego over another. It doesn't have to be about whose ego wins. We can keep the focus on what is fair and right for all concerned, including ourselves.

DASTARDLY DEEDS IN THE DARK

There is worse karma than that for hatred and viciousness. It is the karma for those who are nice to your face but secretly plot your demise. It is worse because the secrecy and manipulativeness of it make it more destructive. The bad karma will manifest at all levels of the person's life as physical, mental, and energetic problems. Of course, if you would like a beautiful life and good karma, then don't be mean, don't be scheming, and, most of all, don't pretend to be good and plot dastardly deeds in the dark!

REJECTION

Do not view rejection as personal failure. There are, at least, two sides involved – ours and the other's. What we want and what the other wants may not be the same. People have a right to be different to us. It is pointless to force anything because freedom of choice is essential for life to flourish. This is the case for both personal and professional. If we face a lot of rejection, in any area of life, then we must look at what we are offering and improve ourselves so that people will want what we have to give.

ENEMIES

- *Question:* I have a situation with betrayal, gossip, malicious plotting, and getting others on her (the enemy's) side. At the same time, the person is smiling directly into my face. How do you respond to someone who lies but appears to be nice and even likes to small talk with you? I don't think it is a good idea to let her know that I see clearly what is going on, but I also don't think it makes sense to appear like nothing is happening.
- *Answer:* People are very commonly just like you described. It is a good opportunity for us to focus on lifting our consciousness into a higher space. As you say, if you tell the person honestly what you can see them doing, it will only make it worse as people do not want to see their own shortcomings. We have to keep practising compassion, seeing that all of this is the normal thing people do out of ignorance and it is all ego driven. Our role in life is to develop to the point where we are not affected by it, we forgive it, we can maintain a peaceful equilibrium, and we can spread the love we feel in our soul. No easy feat!
- *Question:* What is an intelligent way "to spread the love we feel in our soul" (besides the fact that you live it inwardly)? Saying meaningful things, by me, is not allowed by the person or it doesn't help. I feel that small talk is like filling an empty space with empty words. I am mostly quiet and go on

my own way, but that is also not accepted by some other people. The atmosphere is a disturbed one. What would be an intelligent way to deal with it, in a way that we are true to ourself as well as true to the other one?

- *Answer*: I think one would have to be responsive, day by day, to what is wisest with any given person. As you say, the peace inside is first. After that, what is wisest to do or say may vary depending on the receptivity or negativity of the other person. I listen to my own feeling after seeing the person. If I feel bad then I assume there is a lot of ill-will from the person and I protect myself as best I can in the situation. That can change with time. I ask God to help me if I cannot escape the person (and quite often we can't) so that I can stay safe, even if I cannot ever help the other person to change. Often, you can't help them. I also try to work on releasing the anger inside myself about other people's malice. It can take a while. If we keep working on it, it does definitely go.

- *Question:* I need to work on releasing the anger inside. I did say one stupid thing that I regretted. Interestingly, people keep that in mind instead of all the good that has taken place. At the same time, I say to myself that when one works on seeing everything and everyone with a compassionate eye then one can happily be compassionate to oneself.

- *Answer:* Absolutely. We forgive ourselves too. Besides, sometimes it is appropriate to express anger. However, an enemy will look for any little thing to grab onto so we must be aware of that. If

they can't find anything to grab onto then they
will often make something up!

POWER

Although we have goodwill towards everyone, our response to
people needs to be appropriate to the situation. Otherwise, we
can become foolish, weak, conciliatory or naive. If a gentle
word works, wonderful. If not, we may need to be more
direct. If that still doesn't work, spiritually-conscious beings
have a great deal of power backing them to use for the purpose
of protecting the evolution of all that is genuinely good.

BREAK UP AND EVOLUTION

Break-ups, of all kinds, hurt. What is actually breaking up? It
is our concept of what the other person is supposed to do or
be for us. Instead of thinking of the break-up as a loss, we can
see it as evolution. People have a right to choose how they
want to live. That may or may not be in line with us. Either
way, life is in a constant state of evolution and that involves
countless, big-and-little breaking-downs for things to be
made-up, reformed, reborn.

PLAYING WITH IGNORANCE

It takes maturity and unselfishness to handle the complexities
of relationships. Some people, if they do not get what they
want can become a bundle of irrational and malicious intent
set on destroying the perceived cause of their pain. They can
spend years, decades, and even a lifetime or two blaming any
number of people for the injustices they have supposedly
endured. Such are the risks of relationships (of all sorts) with
lesser-evolved people.

BETTER VERSION

When things become challenging, not everyone turns into an enemy. Some people use the opportunity to grow into a better version of themselves. To me, there is nothing more valuable or beautiful than the growth of another's soul. When we have an ear for the Divine then we will be guided. Everyone is cared for, including ourselves. Sometimes, the resulting effect upon someone's life can be quite amazing.

COMMUNICATION

So much of what people say is not what they really think. Lack of authentic communication mostly comes from fear. We must learn how to communicate honestly, and with love. We must also learn how to listen to the constant stream of silent words which ever move between and around us.

GRIEF

Although the advanced spiritual student becomes less and less prone to grief, and incapable of loneliness, nevertheless, they can definitely miss the presence of loved ones who they no longer see. The flower blooms and then dies. Its life and beauty is missed and remembered fondly.

SIDES

When we see life as part of us, and us as part of life, every mistake is our own and every victory is also ours. There are no sides. We are part of every side.

LOVE AND NEED

It is crucial to our relationships that we understand the difference between love and need. If we think we love someone and
they leave, we will blame them for not loving us as much as we
supposedly loved them. If we understand that we may have
needed them more than thy needed us, we might be sad but we
will not blame them. We will make ourselves in such a way
that we need less and love more. Then, no one is likely to leave.
If they do, it will be with our blessing because we will want
them to find their way in life whether it is with us or not.

RIDE IT OUT

You can fall in love with multiple people in life. Ride it out.
You might be married to them or that could be the furthest
thing. The important thing is not the falling in love. Or the
falling out of love. It's the love. Love people. Love them
regardless of their role in your life. And love yourself. Then,
no matter what happens – what you create, what they create,
and what you both create together as two distinct people – it
will somehow work without building up more damaging
karma.

CHILDREN

If we make something beautiful, resilient, alive, strong, gener-
ous, and positive out of our own body, mind, and spirit, then
our life will be impactful. Those who do, find that the
common intense drive to reproduce and create children, in
their own likeness, will significantly lessen. They may still have
children, but the choice will be conscious. While we adore our
children, the most important thing we must leave in this

world, when we die, is the energetic impact of our own life well-lived.

MAKING A HOME

When we are raising children, it is not "making memories" that matters. It is the making of a home. That home is us - the state of our mind and heart. We are what makes the memory of a child. Who we are, who we become as a parent and a person, and how we respond to them and their needs is the most important element in setting them up for their venture into life. When it is time to raise a child, it is time to make ourselves into something as memorable as possible.

OBJECTIVE

My adult daughter finds it amusing (maybe, annoying) that when I speak about her and her sibling's growing up years, I often say something to the effect of, "When I had children..." (implying that I no longer do) or "the children" (not my children). It is a way of saying that child-raising is temporary and that the offspring do not, and never did, belong to me or me to them. It is objectifying, in a good way.

LEADERSHIP

To be a genuine leader means that we dedicate ourself to our people. We don't use people for our own outright or disguised benefit. Our motives – selfish or unselfish – will be intuitively felt (if not obviously known) by most everyone and we will be accordingly trusted or not.

EGO

Because the ego is acutely insecure, it is exclusive and desires to be seen as special. Because the spirit is naturally secure, it is inclusive. It is *ordinary* in an honest, humble, authentic way. Therein lies its power.

DON'T THROW STONES

We should never set ourselves up as the judge of another's character. Far less should we do so based on other people's opinions. Whatever issues we have with someone, we should address with the person, themselves, in a direct but good-willed way. We are all a work-in-progress. Don't hold onto the bad. Keep your eyes on the good, but don't miss an opportunity to help someone see something in a better way. Don't let people hurt you, but neither hurt them.

WILD BEAST SPIRIT

Dahlia could be a formidable foe when fighting for someone she loved, for the protection of someone's soul, or for something important which was worth fighting for. However, by nature, she was a gentle soul. The fighting spirit only seemed to enter her being when she fought for something other than herself. Then, a different force entered her, as if it came from somewhere else. That force had a tendency to not give in until it had fulfilled its mission. As quickly as it appeared, it seemed to retreat back to where it came from until some commanding power directed it to return again.

For many years, Dahlia found the presence of a German shepherd in the house very reassuring. It gave a sense of balance, for the majority of the time when the warrior spirit was elsewhere. However, German shepherds bring their own problems. Instinctively dominant and suspicious, they defend first and ask questions later. They are intensely alert, observant, and intelligent. They live to serve as protector. Of course, these instinctive tendencies have to be modified by strict training or they will take charge of everything and start ruling the world. Given that they are dogs, most of us would prefer that our house is run by relatively civilised human rules rather than dog pack behaviour.

At 50 kilos, Dahlia was a slight thing and would probably have needed another 20 kilos to even have a chance of matching her shepherd's strength. When she walking her dog, it became a mind game. Shepherds are not only highly protective of their whole pack but they will tend to pick their one person that they must protect above all else. When away from this person, they will often refuse to eat, get depressed, and wait for their world to be right again.

When Dahlia walked her shepherd, he would look suspiciously at every cute, white, fluff-ball dog as if it was a possible threat to her life. And so, the walks were a matter of her continuously insisting that she was in charge and, *We will do it my way.* In his mind, he could have it all sorted out so very quickly!

Everything comes at a price. Dahlia paid for the comfort of her shepherd's protectiveness by having to contain his *wild beast* spirit so that there were no casualties.

COLOUR

Conversations - funny, touching, ridiculous, wise, and real - give us important moments along the way. While it is true that our happiness is our own making, it is also true that so much of the colour, brilliance, and interest of life comes from our connection to other people.

COMPETITION

Healthy competition is not detrimental to our well-being and progress. It is advantageous. It helps us to recognise the weaker areas within ourselves that need improvement.

SUSPICIOUS AND VICIOUS

The ego, when it is pacified, is still suspicious. When it is alert with danger, it quickly becomes vicious. Neither be that ego nor let other people's viciousness destroy you. The spirit is a mighty defence. It gives a shield which makes the insults of the ego meaningless. It gives peace by keeping our eyes not on the ego of others but on their inner being which is neither suspicious nor vicious. Just like us, their inner being belongs to the Divine although, at the moment, they may have a hard time seeing that.

ALLIANCES

Be careful who you make alliances with. A relationship which will prove NOT to be beneficial to you will be marked with secretiveness, withholding, flimsy promises, possessiveness, exclusivity, and emotional rollercoaster rides. While you can love a person in this state, they, in return, can neither see nor understand your love. On the other hand, beneficial relationships are built on happiness, openness, sincerity, peacefulness, and equilibrium. Such alliances welcome, with open arms, the sunlight-glow of everything touched with genuine, simple love.

HOW DID HE EVER FIND YOU?

The Manhattan hairdresser asked with genuine intrigue, "But, darling, how did your husband ever find you in Australia?"

Amy could see that he was envisaging Mervin setting off, from the States, on a quest to find his wife-to-be and, against all odds, finding her amongst the wild kangaroos of outback Australia. There was more than a little truth in it. Amy laughed.

Mervin was everything that Amy was not: sophisticated, wealthy, and worldly-wise. If it had not been for his mid-life crisis and a conscientious effort at finding a spiritual path, neither would ever have come into contact with the other.

After significant professional success, and a few failed marriages, Mervin decided that his move to Australia would be an opportunity to find a new direction in life. He was serious in his quest. A very quick and sharp intellect guaranteed that he read every trailblazing spiritual and psychological book on the market. After friending young Amy, at a spiritual meeting, they found that they shared a love of deep thinking and literature.

Amy's first visit to Mervin's apartment was pivotal. It wasn't because of a passionate love affair. It was more of a love affair with his books. As Amy walked hesitantly into his lavish hallway, she stopped, in her tracks, at the rows of beautiful books lining the wall. It only took a moment for Amy to realise that all the books she had ever wanted to read were right there, waiting for her with outstretched hands. It was true bliss. The time-honoured wisdom of Buddha, Lao-Tzu, St. Francis of Assisi, Ramakrishna, and Meister Eckhart; the founding psychologists Freud, Jung, Maslow, and Erickson; the new thought of Mary Baker Eddy, Blavatsky, Rudolph Steiner, and Ernest Holmes; the inspiration of Kahlil Gibran, C.S. Lewis, and Edgar Cayce; the transpersonal psychology of

Abraham Maslow, Carl Rogers, Ken Wilber, and Thomas Hora; the Bible, the Bhagavad Gita, and other sacred texts. The door had been grandly opened and it was irresistible and undeniable.

When Amy was a young teenager, she would often go into the Christian bookshop, near the train station, on the way home from school. She didn't have enough money to buy even one book in all the time she went there. She told herself patiently that, one day, she would have money to buy hundreds of books. She decided which ones she would buy at the shop and then walked out the door. The volunteer shop assistants would smile kindly at her and wonder what a girl her age was thinking amongst the books. Before the internet, books meant knowledge, and Amy knew that knowledge could be turned into wisdom.

Amy and Mervin both came to the relationship with the best of intentions. Amy felt that she had found a spiritual and intellectual soulmate. Although, of course, money is a very useful thing, she was not overly interested in Mervin's money. In fact, she felt that a lot of money was very alienating.

Some years later, when walking with her little children and her aunt through an orchard, Amy's aunt casually, but poignantly, mentioned, "You know Amy, it is generally not first-generation rich people who have the problem. They can usually remember where they came from. It is the second generation."

She did not say what *the problem* was, but the words spoilt, delusional, and obnoxious sprang to Amy's mind.

Nevertheless, the money did bring many experiences which otherwise would have been totally inaccessible. For this, Amy was grateful. She found Mervin at just the right moment in his life. However, she did not realise that it was but a moment, and a long way from being sustainable for him.

Mervin felt that he had found in Amy a real chance to have

a loving family. Kind, nurturing, and intelligent, she was a true find. As she was young, she had little baggage from life and Mervin believed that together they could start from scratch and create the family life he longed for.

As life would have it, Mervin's mid-life honesty and commitment lasted not more than a few, short years and was not found again until, many decades later, his closing years would rediscover it in very different financial and personal circumstances. Found once, life-commitment is never as difficult to find as the first time.

The relationship gave Amy exceptional opportunities. It turned her into a woman. It gave her experiences which she could never have dreamed up. It gave her culture. Amy previously knew nothing of music or the arts or the world at large. It even gave her a new language and a more sophisticated way of speaking. It gave her an experience of wealth so that she knew it would never be necessary to feel less than anyone, and God help her if she ever thought anyone less than her. She could handle money if it came her way, and not chase it if it did not. She had lived in a world much older than herself and it changed her. It made her much older than her years. Strangely, after its completion, she found that, unlike her younger years when she craved the friendship of much older people, she now sincerely enjoyed the company of younger people (knowing their limitations, but not needing them to be more than they could be).

The whole relationship was a blessing, regardless of its long, drawn out, and lonely demise. It was a blessing, but it was more of a blessing when it was over.

MAGNIFY

If we look for the faults in others, we will certainly find them. If we keep our eyes on the beauty and goodness in others, it will magnify it in them and us.

DESIRABLE

If we want people to love us, it's not about making ourselves into a more attractive, likeable, desirable creature. It's about making ourselves into a more loving being. It's not about us at all. It's about the genuine needs of other people. The problem of not being loved will be solved. Further, the very question of whether we are loved or not will disappear from our thought processes.

SHARING

Whatever we would like to make stronger in ourselves will be strengthened by sharing it with others. When we share, we gain. When we withhold, we lose. When we give away, we keep. When we hold tightly, we are left with nothing.

APOLOGETIC BEGGAR AND KARMA

I was at a car-wash when a man came up and asked me for 10c for the machine. It was one of those car-wash places that recognises neither rich nor poor. You had to have exactly the right coins or it wouldn't work. It didn't take credit cards. It did have a change machine, but the change machine was as fussy as the car wash machine and often didn't work properly.

The man looked stressed and said that he was late and the change machine wouldn't take his money and that all he needed was 10c more. I gave him a coin and off he went. A minute later, he was back asking, like an apologetic beggar, to borrow a dollar because "the damn thing wants another dollar!" I gave it to him.

As I finished washing my car, a beautiful, new, black Mercedes pulled up next to me and the window went down. There was the man, far from beggar-mode.

He handed me his business card and said, "I run a car hire company. If you need a car, you can call me."

With many thank-yous, he drove off waving.

That was good value for a dollar, I thought.

POWER OF LOVE

Falling in love with someone only has so much power. It's a lot, but eventually the person has to want to grow. Falling in love is a powerful inroad into change, but, in the end, it won't be enough on its own. It is never enough. People have to have a willingness to want to truly love, to change, to understand things better. Without that, no relationship survives and thrives in a functional, happy way.

SWIMMING IN LOVE

If we see ourselves as living within the context of love, as swimming in an ocean of love, then we can be more relaxed about the flow of love in life – where it comes from and where it goes. Sometimes, it will move towards us. Sometimes, it will move away from us. All the while, we are still swimming and the water of love surrounds us. So, we can relax. We become love; no asking for it, not manipulating it, not afraid that it will leave. We become it, and anytime someone else wishes to join that flow of love, we are grateful and glad.

FULL FLOWER

We all want sweetness, beauty, harmony, exhilaration, and happiness in our lives. Don't search for it, endlessly and fruitlessly, in other people and circumstances. Become it yourself. Become it with total commitment and in full force. Your life will flower with tremendous potential.

BENEVOLENCE

When we look at people benevolently, we see them as what they are capable of, not as what they are necessarily demonstrating right now.

ACCEPTANCE

Love begins with an acceptance of the person as they are. That does not mean that we accept bad behaviour or a lazy attitude towards life. It means that our primary focus is on loving the person, come what may. Part of love is helping them to become the best that they can be. We want the best for them, but our love is not dependent on it. Life, without any assistance from us, has its own teaching methods.

LOVING FOCUS

In every situation in which we find ourselves, we should keep our thoughts on, "What can I give to this person? To this group? To this situation?" Such a focus will naturally make our energy field loving, regardless of our personality, what is said, or what is done. A person whose honest intention is to love will always be wanted in life. We may not be wanted where we want to be wanted, but Life, itself, will unfailingly want us.

FAMILY UNIT

I envisage a world where family units will be more fluid. It's not that the concept of family will be disrespected or that it will disintegrate, but the reasons for the formation and continuation of the family unit (which is the base unit of one's personal life) will be broader and more fluid than are currently common. Generally, the formation of the unit comes from physical needs and also the drive to create children. We should respect our biological make-up, however, in a more evolved world, the desire to procreate will be less because people will have so many other outlets for creation and loving connection. In a more evolved world, the body's physical drives will not be the motivating factor for forming units of energy capable of doing so much more than providing basic needs. When people couple, form families, and form groups, they are creating energy units. When seen as energy units, the reasons for formation and what we can create become infinitely bigger and endlessly fascinating.

IT WAS ONLY NATURAL

Emerson was a man who didn't cry about himself. He cried at movies. That was other people's lives. He was used to carrying on with his responsibilities. However, this particular day, he was sobbing.

Millie hugged him and said, "I'm so sorry, Emerson. We have been friends so long. I know you want us to be together, but I feel that we are better as friends."

Although apologetic for crying, Emerson kept crying. After many years of weariness in his personal life, he finally had the opportunity to be with someone he wanted to be with. He also knew that in order to move into the next stage of his life, he would need to change many things and those around him wouldn't like it. Courage wasn't his strong point. He was good. He wasn't brave. Millie said that she would help him, as a friend, but he felt that it would not be enough. He was probably right. He loved Millie but, more than that, he needed her. He felt that he was so close to getting what he wanted, but her answer was still no.

It didn't take long for Millie and Emerson to start talking again after the difficult discussion about being friends not lovers. They had been friends for so many years that it was only natural to talk again. They returned to seeing each other as much as before, if not more. Millie didn't say no to Emerson again. She let the lover-relationship happen. He was a good man. He deserved the help. The relationship was easily compatible. They were both easy to live with. However, the worth of a relationship is not based on ease, but on purpose and depth.

Emerson came from a controlling family and community. Were they controlling? Actually, they were just normal people. Anyone can turn into a tyrant if we let them. Even the most inoffensive of dogs can become a monster, in their own home, if their master becomes a servant to them, afraid to take the lead.

In fact, Emerson owned just such a tyrant dog – a little Maltese called Poppet. The dog had been a lone and loved canine member of her family for twelve years. To mention a few problems: she would bite anyone whenever it suited her, refuse to eat anything but what she fancied at the moment, would not go through the dog-flap unless someone opened it for her, and would sleep on whichever bed she wished to (biting the bed occupant's feet if he or she dared to move in a way which annoyed her.) With all the pampering, fussing, and loving, she was a mental mess. She would shake uncontrollably at everything and nothing, was depressed and anxious, and would alienate herself from humans by barking at and biting anyone she did not trust which was, pretty much, everyone. As for her relationship with other dogs? Dogs?

"There are no dogs but me. I do not even see them."

Is spoiling someone (or some dog) love? No, it creates problem after problem for those who live the illusion that life rotates around them; that they are entitled. Many well-meaning dog owners are big on loving the dog first. If you tell them that dogs need rules, a lot of people believe it's going to hurt their dog. In fact, dogs need you to be the pack leader or they get insecure or delusional. Either way, there are problems. Millie and Poppet had some world-class battles for head of the pack position. Eventually, Poppet surrendered and her anxiety and depression disappeared.

If we are good but not strong, we must learn that without courage other people will destroy our life. Everything we value is open to being taken or destroyed by a stronger person. If we are strong but not good, we must learn that without goodness, we destroy our own life.

At every turn, the supposed-tyrants, in Emerson's family and community, were challenged; not by Emerson, but by Millie. Millie knew that if she didn't stand her ground, not only would Emerson remain imprisoned but, once she was committed to the relationship, she would become the next victim. As soon as one tyrant was put in its place, another appeared. It only took a little while for all the would-be tyrants to join forces to try and recapture their lost territory. People with many different reasons can become allies to face a supposed enemy. People will fight hard not to lose whatever it was they got out of previously captured territory.

In the early stages, Emerson did his part (which mostly just to stand there). Eventually, it became obvious that Emerson and Millie were not conceding defeat and so the enemies retreated. Emerson relaxed, thought the battle was over, and congratulated himself on doing a good job. That was a fatal mistake. The enemy simply bided their time, regrouped, and came in with a new approach. If you cannot win by insults, you can often win by compliments. Compliments can do what insults cannot. That was the beginning of the end.

They were not difficult battles for Millie. On her own, she could have handled them quickly. A no which means no is a formidable defence in any situation. However, she wasn't on her own. When one helps another to fight their battles, the problem is generally not the thing that is fought, but the person one is helping to stand their ground. For every house that was secured, Emerson would unwittingly open a door and two windows.

We have to learn how to defend ourself, our truth, our gifts, and that which is precious to us. We mustn't open the doors and windows to thieves of happiness. Emerson loved Millie as much as he could love any woman. He loved her, but he loved his safety more.

And so, Millie spoke to Emerson as soon as she felt he could bear to hear it, and said, "If you cannot protect yourself, how can you ever protect me? You will let them destroy us both rather than own your own truth."

Self-preservation kicked in, and Millie left. She and Emerson remained good friends. They had been friends so long; it was only natural.

RECEPTIVITY

God does not need our love to be complete. However, when we do not communicate with the Divine, when we are too busy with our own problems, and when we don't trust that the Creator is there, then the channels to God are blocked and creation is incomplete. The more attentive we are, the more God seems to pay attention to us.

In the same way, one of the factors which will determine

where and to whom we give our energy and love is the presence or absence of receptivity. Does the person value our being in their life? Do they listen to and think about what we say? Do they give us their time? Do they give us part of their heart? We don't need it all but, if we are to have an impact on another being, we need a real part of it.

GOOD ENOUGH

Many people feel *not good enough* for certain people in their life. We must get to the point of realising it all comes from inside us; not outside. Otherwise, we will be forever reaching upwards to the wrong thing. We will be trying to make ourselves safer by attaching to people who we believe are stronger than us. We need to find that strong centre inside ourselves, then other people will not feel we want to use them for our own purposes.

GROWING CIRCLE

If we want to be seen as a loving person, we can't just act loving. We have to actually care. Most everyone can sense the difference between a genuinely caring person and one who is not. To care is to empathise. The capacity to empathise is a developmental stage. We have to feel secure enough within ourselves that we can turn our attention to the problems and joys of other people. We realise that what happens in the life of another has a meaningful impact on our own. The more developed our consciousness becomes, the larger the circle of those we care about.

POINT OF VIEW

If we see ourselves primarily from the point of view of our relationships (good, bad, and ugly), we will never be able to reach our full potential. While we deeply love those God gives us along the way, the most important, ongoing relationship we will ever have is with our own Divine being. We were born as a single entity, we will face death on our own, and we must make our way back to the Divine under our own steam. Never give that right and responsibility away to another person, and never take it from another. You will find that the respect and gratitude from those you do this for runs deep.

SAME THING

Love is our greatest need – giving it and receiving it. Our task is to learn how to do both beautifully until, one day, giving and receiving will be the same thing.

THANKS, LOVE

It was Anzac Day. In Australia, that is when servicemen and women are remembered and honoured. It is also when the shops don't open till 1 p.m. As it's a once-a-year phenomenon, people often forget. I, along with a growing collection of citizens, stood outside the local supermarket waiting for it to open. The local homeless man sat next to the entrance, ready for donations. He probably isn't homeless but I can't call him a beggar because he is too polite and dignified. He has a profession – he asks for money.

"Got a few spare coins, love?" he always asks.

If you say no, he doesn't object.

If you give him something, he always says, "Thanks, love."

I was at the head of the supermarket line.

When I first came up to the un-opening automatic doors, the man said, "Not open for fifteen more minutes. Anzac Day, love."

I noticed that he gave other people the same response. Not everyone. Some people he said nothing to.

An equally scruffy man arrived as a shopper. He was probably sixty but, like the homeless man, wore the scars of a hard sixty years. He seemed to know the homeless man and chatted with him after he was told about the supermarket's current closure.

The shopper looked at the homeless man and said, "So, when are you open mate?"

Without hesitation, the homeless man replied, "24/7. I'm always open."

"You're keen," said his shopping friend.

Neither changed tone, neither cracked a smile, but both had cracked a joke, and shared it with all listening.

After a pause, the homeless man turned to me and said, "Got much to buy today, love?"

"Not much," I answered with a smile.

"What's on your list?" he asked.

"I'll tell you," I said pulling my list out with a dramatic flurry.

I was fairly sure that he didn't really want me to read through my boring list.

"Butter," I said and paused to see if that was enough.

He nodded encouragingly to go on.

"Eggs," I continued with another pause.

"Yes," he said with great interest as if I was reading him the most enthralling story.

By now, everyone else was also listening to my shopping list.

"Chocolate," I said with an enthusiastic wave of my arms.

That one was greeted with much approval.

At the end of my list reading, the shopping mate said to the homeless man, "All I heard was chocolate."

We all parted company with the opening of the door. A man, I didn't recognise, passed me near the eggs and smiled in acknowledgment of the pre-shopping exchange.

On my way out of the supermarket, I gave the homeless man the chocolate I had bought him and a little bit of cash.

"Thanks, love," he said putting the money in his dirty plastic bag.

He looked at the chocolate and repeated, "Thanks, love. Thanks a lot."

CHAPTER 3

Spiritual Path

ENTIRELY SELFISH

NO MARTYRS

When I was fourteen, a missionary visited my school and gave a little talk. Although I can't remember what she said, I do remember being impressed with her as a person. I couldn't put it into words but there was something special about her. It might have been the calm look in her eyes even though, from what she said, her life was far from calm. Certainly, I recognised a very unselfish attitude and she seemed happy without trying to convince anyone that she was.

After the talk, a student I didn't know approached me and said, "I think you are going to be a missionary."

I was surprised. At that age, I was shy and introverted. There was nothing for her to gain by going to the trouble of telling me.

"No," I said, "I don't think so."

It seemed to me that even if one did want to be a missionary, it wasn't the sort of thing that one would admit to. Although the girl didn't appear to have any intention of repeating the conversation, I was well aware that the teenage world can be brutal.

"I saw the look in your eyes when the missionary was talking," said the girl by way of explanation. "I was watching you."

I must have been so absorbed in the missionary's talk that I didn't notice her watching. What the girl said was surprising and thought-provoking, but it wasn't frightening. However, the next thing she said did frighten me.

"I also think you will be a martyr," she said in the same matter-of-fact manner.

As we weren't friends, her prediction of my fatal, if not glorious, future didn't seem to bother her in the slightest. She walked off and for the rest of our schooling days, we never crossed paths again.

At the time (and over the years whenever her comment came to mind), I told myself that the girl knew nothing. However, something in what she said stayed me. It wouldn't have scared me if I thought there wasn't some truth in it. In my heart, I knew that if it came down to someone else's life and my own, I would probably have to choose the other or I wouldn't be able to live with myself. I was, indeed, likely material for martyrdom. Of course, I didn't want to be a martyr. Who wants to die? I didn't want to sacrifice my life or happiness or talents or anything. Who would?

Eventually, I noticed that the thought of martyrdom had disintegrated in my consciousness. Thankfully, it happened before I decided to take up the call! I learned from my spiritual studies and from my life practices that, contrary to an unconscious belief that God wants us to suffer, the Divine wants us to be happy. My young fellow-student was responding to the belief that people who love God make big sacrifices and see other people's lives as being more important than their own and act accordingly.

Sacrifice is not the way of the higher spiritual teachings.

We learn that there is no value in it. There is only value in healing, peace, and seeing life aright. God doesn't want martyrs. The Divine wants the expression of its own harmonious, creative, and beautiful being. That sounds happy, right? The only thing we sacrifice is the ego. And that is no sacrifice when we realise how flawed, troublesome, and destructive it is.

No one has to be a martyr. On the contrary, everyone should be entirely selfish. Not selfish in the normal sense of the word, but selfish in the way of knowing that the spiritual path means we value everything which adds to our own well-being. When we love, we live with connectedness. When we forgive, we feel stress-free. When we create, we live with inspiration. When we follow our inner direction, we feel alive. Is that even a choice?

PURPOSE OF LIFE

We must strengthen, expand, and extend the energetic systems of our own being. It takes inner work and commitment. We must work with every level of our being to make it more harmonious, in tune, more efficient, more effective. That is the purpose of life.

GROWTH

Growth is formed in the hidden deep. Below the surface, everything can be made into food for the push upwards. What matters is the springing forth, not the sinking deep. We must learn to look for the flowering in other people, not the mess from which it is born.

ISOLATION

In spite of any indication to the contrary, you can never be disconnected from the invisible, irrevocable, ever-present connections of Love. You are loved. You are here for a purpose. Your life is unique, important, and irreplaceable.

BLOOMING

Fulfilment on the path of personal growth does not mean to become more like someone we admire. It means to become a more fully flowering version of ourselves.

LIGHT BEARERS

I first learned hands-on-healing when I was twenty and belonged to a Catholic Charismatic Community. It was one of my favourite things to do. I never doubted its authenticity because, to me, it seemed obviously real and beneficial.

I remember attending a community conference in a different state. At that stage, I didn't have any money and was gifted the conference and flight tickets which I was thrilled about. The conference was a large, enthusiastic gathering with many hundreds of young adults fired up with spiritual energy.

One hands-on-healing session had a particularly long line. I waited patiently for my turn with the prayer-healers. They were not much more than girls, about my age, but very sincerely doing their best. As I knelt for them to put their hands on my shoulders, I told myself that it didn't matter whose hands were on me because the power of God was running through them. I raised my arms and turned my palms and head Heavenwards. It was a beautiful moment of light. Afterwards, I thanked the girls and happily trot off.

Later on, in the bathroom, I overheard one of my friends say to another friend, "Two of the healers asked me who our friend is. I told them her name is Donna and asked why they wanted to know. They said that when they prayed for her, they were surrounded by a powerful, beautiful light. They said that there was something special about Donna's calling. Do you think we should tell her?"

They did tell me because they were lovely girls. I thanked them and, as I didn't want to make a fuss about it, I changed the conversation to something else.

This experience has always stayed in the back of my mind. I remember the profound feeling of light when I was being prayed for. I also remember that it was very affirming, at that age, to have strangers acknowledge my calling. A spiritually oriented person, in our earthly world, has to put up with a lot of misalignment.

HAPPINESS

If we are happy when we are alone then we must be in good company. Take that good company to other people. Whether they appreciate it or not is their decision, but make sure you are part of the path to happiness, not part of the path to suffering.

PROBLEMS

Our problems seem many and infinitely varied. They are not even resolved before new ones arise. No one could solve or foresee them all. Fortunately, they all stem from the same tree and can be handled with one fix. They grow from the tree of separation. If we plant ourselves securely in the right soil, our problems will be seen in a different light and will, quite often, disappear. What is that right soil? It cannot be taught. It is felt. It is intuitively understood. It is seen. Eventually, it is the only way of seeing that makes any sense.

WHO WALKS BESIDE US

When we remember who walks beside us, everything we touch, everything we gaze upon, everything we turn our attention to has the inner light of creation. Nothing we do can fail in that light of love and grace.

SAFETY

Walk safely in the knowledge of who walks with you, but do not be reckless. Be aware of everything, but don't beware.

GRACE

Grace is a gentle thing. Easily destroyed by selfishness, envy, ill will, and fear. Easily invited by kindness, hope, forgiveness, and love.

LIGHT

The spiritual path is not a burden when it improves our life greatly.

For my yoke is easy and my burden is light.

— JESUS

EVOLUTION AND TEACHER

At some stage in our evolution, our being can have a certain unrelenting pain which will not be relieved by conventional means. A particular sort of person may then enter our life. That person becomes our spiritual teacher. At first, we may not know that they are that. However, after a while, we will see that their words and presence are substantially changing us in a positive way. Whether intended or not, they have become a teacher to us. Alternatively, if we realise that someone has a negative impact on our life, then we should access how much contact we have with that person.

MYSTICISM

Mysticism is only mysterious when we don't yet understand the world beyond the physical. Then, it's not mysterious - it is common sense. Perhaps, not common to everyone, but common to those on the spiritual path.

PEACE

There is no greater gift than the heart that can transmit peace. By sharing it, we keep it.

GATHERING OURSELVES

Many things happen in our communities, families, work, and world. We have little choice about most of them. But we have total choice about what is inside us. Happiness develops within our own being; not from outside influences. It is crucial to have time alone to develop this inner awareness of happiness and stability – a few minutes, an hour, a day, a week. We are not gathering more of the world in that space, but gathering ourselves into a clear, calm, loving being capable of doing much.

LIFE EXPERIENCE

If we would like our life experience to improve, we mustn't focus on: how do I get people to like me better, appreciate me more, or give me more of what I want? We must focus on: how do I turn myself into a more loving being, and one who is using as much of their potential as possible in this lifetime? To be loving is not a sacrifice. It is to become more connected with the strong, compassionate, energetic, intelligent source of our existence.

STAY AWAKE

If we are awake, we can safely and happily go with the flow. If we are asleep, the flow can easily lead us into a nightmare.

NATURE OF THE EGO

The nature of our ego is to try and turn every situation, every conversation, and every interaction into something which benefits itself. Without conscious discipline, we are far more selfish and far more uncaring than we acknowledge. This is not an indictment or an accusation. It is simply the way it is. When we become more aware of the beauty within us and of our place in this incredible, miraculous life then our attention is pulled away from building up our egos in an ineffective and pathetic attempt to be somebody. We are already everything we could ever wish to be.

HAPPY GAME

Whether life blesses us or torments us, plays with us or abuses us, kisses us or destroys us is our own choice. Choose to be blessed and kissed, and you will be part of a happy game.

OURS TO ANSWER

Charismatics and Pentecostals generally place their hands on the person's shoulders. If we add to that the Eastern knowledge of chakras, it becomes a small step for the healer to place the hands directly on the body's various energy centres, as in Reiki. It goes without saying that the healer must have the capacity to heal or, more precisely, the capacity to let the healing channel flow through them. Otherwise, to the client, it can feel like an invasion of personal boundaries or like nothing.

Before being a full-time author, I had a private practice as a spiritual healer and counsellor, for about ten years, in which I practised, among other things, hands-on healing. Healing is partly a selfish career, as the path must always be. I wanted to learn how to be completely healthy and happy myself. Of course, I also wanted to share what I hopefully found with a world which seemed deeply in need of it. Healer and author, John Hargreaves, who was a spiritual teacher of mine, at that stage, was particularly supportive of me starting a practice as a healer. He said,

When we understand our oneness with God, we are able to heal spiritually because we know that in divine reality, there is no human concept of anything or anybody to fix up. The more clearly we realise this, the more the human scene becomes subservient and harmonious. It falls into line with the overriding power and completeness of the infinite All.

— JOHN HARGREAVES

In normal everyday life, I do not generally move into other people's energy fields. Firstly, it is too intrusive. One has to be invited. Secondly, I wouldn't last very long. Constantly merging with other people's unbalanced energy fields would be exhausting. One has to only answer what is ours to answer.

Sometimes, when working with a healer, a person can heal instantly. Whatever problem they came in with can disappear before they walk out the door. In such situations, it is a combination of the person's openness, the previous working-through of the problem, the capability of the healer to connect with the healing forces, and destiny. People often seek help at the tipping point of a problem when it seems the darkest, but actually dawn is just over the horizon.

The timing of a healing is neither the healer's concern nor the client's. We do our best and the rest is up to things beyond our control. Definitely, if we keep moving in the healing direction, things will change in a beneficial way and we will grow in many ways we would not have imagined. The intention to get well adds much fuel to our progress.

The ability to heal (both ourself and others) comes automatically to all serious spiritual students, once they reach a certain point in their evolution. Ultimately, our soul is in the healing hands of the Divine. They are the majestic, invisible hands of healing which moulded our form and which continue to nurture our spirit.

BEST BARGAIN

For everything in life, there is a price. The trouble is that most people pay dearly for worthless things. On the path of wisdom, we still have to pay, at various stages, but as soon as we do, we realise that nothing of any value was taken from us. Indeed, everything is given to us. There's no better bargain.

STRUGGLE

We struggle to find peace within ourselves and with each other, but all the struggle disappears in those moments of acceptance, trust, and love. It disappears into nothingness as if it was all totally unnecessary. Yet, without the struggle, we could not have known the choice.

CHANGE

It takes a mammoth effort to change, but the difference it makes to our happiness makes it worth the effort.

THIS MOMENT

If we accept life as it is, at this moment; people as they are, at this moment; situations as they are, at this moment, we only have to endure the bad things once. Otherwise, we constantly rerun painful experiences and experience them a thousand times over in our mind. Acceptance of what is, at this moment, helps us to think clearly and calmly which gives us more ability to change situations for the better.

WOO-WOO

I have little tolerance for woo-woo sort of spiritual people who imagine, and generally quite loudly proclaim, their specialness. Yet, invariably, if you look at their lives, they are failing on many levels - relationships, finance, professional success, and mental stability. They are usually emotionally insecure, and often mentally unstable. Give me a sane, clear, motivated, intense, "unspiritual" person any day! The spiritual path is not woo-woo. It is very realistic and practical. It's just that it is dealing with different dimensions and one has to have an awareness of what is in those dimensions to know what is realistic and practical there.

By their fruits, you will know them.

— JESUS

INSIDE

First, we must become firmly established within ourselves and then we can move out into the world. If we try to establish ourselves from the outside (with career, achievements, relationships to certain people), we will feel that we are constantly chasing ourselves and it will not end well. Many people start out with a passion for something and because it is not securely grounded internally, they end up feeling like it is draining the life out of them! Every day, we need to meet ourselves on the inside. It is a completely private matter. There is no one to impress; no one to applaud. Neither is there anyone to disapprove. Who do we meet? Our higher self, our better self, the self who knows, without doubt, why we are here. Whatever we create from the inside will carry an unshakeable and positive energy above and beyond our own doing. It will be blessed.

ALONE

The spiritual path can be scary for many people because you have to walk it alone. You don't have to be without people in your life. You can be married, and you can be part of highly interactive groups. However, such relationships are human arrangements based on the most pressing of our own and other people's needs. Nothing wrong with that. That is how healthy relationships form - from the basis of satisfying, at least, a reasonable amount of our needs in a viable and maintainable way. If you are fortunate, those arrangements will be blessed and beneficial.

We mustn't confuse the spiritual, inner domain with the external, worldly domain. Both are important. After all, you didn't come here for nothing. However, if you are ready to develop yourself at a different level, you need to get used to being alone. The inner world can only be travelled solitarily even if another person holds our hand the entire time. Give yourself periods of solitude. How else can you learn to not only be comfortable but thriving on the spiritual path?

HUMILITY

Without humility, we can never know the subtler, beautiful, fear-free things of life. We may know success, power, money, control, social and professional standing. But we will not know love, compassion, the look of peace in another's eyes, the collapse of self when watching the profound dignity of the ocean. For these things require our absence as a God and our presence as one made by One.

ANGELS FROM THE DUST

I come from a family of outback Australian farmers. My Grandfather was a pioneer farmer. His son, and eventually his grandson, were also farmers. As children, we spent many carefree, unrestrained holidays enjoying farm life. My father died when I was in my last year of school and my uncle, who was running the family farm, kindly took it upon himself to be our proxy father. He knew that my father was very proud that I would be going to university and he watched with interest to see how my great professional career would unfold. He was not impressed to find out that one of my main jobs after graduating from university was teaching religion in schools.

I recall him throwing his arms in the air and, storming out of the room in exasperation, said, *"Religion? Religion! What sort of a job is that? Teaching Hail Mary's!"*

There was no point trying to explain my point of view. He felt that I was throwing away my good mind, my education, and my talents. He did the same when I spent much of my time working voluntarily with the poor and forgotten "street people" of inner Sydney. He felt someone else could look after them and that I was wasting my life. I never dared to tell him that, at one point, I seriously considered joining a religious order of nuns. That would have been the end. He probably knew anyway.

The Australian outback culture would not perhaps be the first choice for someone destined for a very strong spiritual path. Spirituality and the outback are not a natural marriage. Nevertheless, it was so.

To balance things out, I also recall another story. One day, the mother of that uncle, when she was quite elderly, was hanging out clothes on the old wire clothes line held up by branches. She looked up from the vast dusty earth into the vast blue sky and saw the image of a face in the clouds. She said that she did not know if it was an angel or me but it made her feel much better. She died not long after that.

PURITY

Devotion makes everything and everyone beautiful. The purity of devotion brings out the inner beauty of all. One can be devoted to anything good and it will have the same effect.

SPEAKING

Say less, but mean more with what you say. It's a practice; a discipline. It will make you more aware. Your presence will become more beneficial.

MEDITATION

Meditation is not some new-age mumbo-jumbo for ungrounded people. True meditation is intelligent, humble, and powerful. It means to become consciously alive and well – to heal our body, to clear our mind, and to free our spirit. In this way, we reduce (and often eliminate) our problems and we have the deep satisfaction of living in an ever-evolving, connected, and creative way.

WITHDRAWAL

When things are not going well in our life, it is a good time to withdraw into a safe place and drop a layer of our being. Traditionally, that is what ashrams and monasteries are for – a supported environment where it is safe to go within, explore oneself, and shed some of the damaging karma and thought processes. If we so desire, we can make our own safe place. We can learn how to protect ourselves from negative thinking, harmful people, and counter-productive environments. We can align with whatever will help us to create less suffering. We, thus, become cleaner, brighter, and more willing to take up the endless possibilities of life.

GETTING BIGGER

We need to expand ourselves. Get bigger. Not body-bigger, but the light-that-radiates-from-within-us-bigger. The healthier and more harmonious our being is on the different levels – physical, mental, emotional, energetic – the greater will be the light which radiates from us. We will become more impactful, beneficial, and creative with less effort. Less effort, but more effective intention of effort.

PRACTICE

Make a sacred space out of your own body, mind, and spirit. Refine it every day with whatever practices work best for you. Don't ignore one aspect of your being out of laziness, ignorance, resentment or resistance.

MADE STRONGER

Wherever you are with your growth, share that with the world in ways that are natural and enjoyable to you. Everything we share is made stronger in our own being.

CHOOSE HAPPINESS

We can choose to be happy. We can choose to be free. We do not have to accept the bonds which feed sadness. We do not have to bow before the ones who ask us to smile while they destroy us. We can choose life and peace. Happiness is not an accident. It is a deliberate decision. Someone else cannot choose it for us. We must choose it ourselves. We must align our lives with what we truly value, connect with those who also value that, and disconnect from those who don't.

EXPANDING AND CONTRACTING

When we are happy, our instinct is to expand. When we are afraid, our instinct is to contract. At least, in the contractions, find the thread of beauty and strength which will eventually lead to the right sort of expansion.

LOOKING AND CHANGING

There is always another way of looking at things. All change begins with the realisation that things can be different. Without that concept, the seed of change will not be nourished.

FAILURE

The making of the person is not how we fail but in how we recover.

ABSOLUTE

Be devoted to something – anything good. The process of being absolutely dedicated to anything positive will transform you, your life, and your environment.

INDIVIDUAL

The world is changed by change in individuals. It's not the world that needs changing. It's us.

HESITATION

Life travels along, without stopping, regardless of whether we hesitate or not. Many things change in life for all of us. Every day, every year is important.

PRUNING

Where our focus is, so too is our development. When a plant is pruned, its inner eye is on the area which has been cut and it puts all its energy into that part of itself. Thus, a pruned plant will produce abundant growth where it has been pruned.

WILLING TO SHARE

If we are willing to share – people, money, talents, the limelight, kind-heartedness – we will, one way or another, always have what we need in life. If we try to own people, hold onto money, hog the limelight, are too scared to express our talents, or are stingy with our love then life will have a hard time giving us much more than sorrow.

SIGHT

If we can see the little things, we can see the entire universe.

THE MIND

Be helpful without being condescending. The mind condescends because it is insecure. The spirit has its eyes on sharing whatever will make joyful, clean, and light.

START THE DAY

Start the day right by talking to your best friend - the Divine. Better still; don't talk, just listen. Best of all; don't do anything, simply be together. That way, your Friend has the most opportunity to reclaim your consciousness so that your day will be maximally happy and least karmic-gathering. A moment of true togetherness will wipe out all your hurts, worries, and fears. That moment will join with many other moments, and your life will be one of grace.

BREATHING

Prayer is like breathing. Always there. Life-giving. Healing. Revitalising. Stabilising. Connecting us to the Source.

ENLARGED BORDERS

There are many paths to God. Some never mention God. No matter. What matters is that the path leads to increasing mental clarity, emotional freedom, physical wholeness, and energetic vibrancy. It matters that we know what we are supposed to do, and with whom. It matters that our sense of responsibility expands out from ourselves, beyond our immediate loved ones, beyond our individual communities, out into the whole of humanity.

ATTENTION

We must learn the fine art of paying complete attention to life without holding onto it. Children naturally want to play with life. Although we must grow up and take our rightful place in the world as adults, the trick is to regain the lightness of a happy, secure child. Far more secure than the variable nature of humanness is the security of the Divine parent. It not only dreamt us into existence but guides us through life and then, one day, after enough play, gladly takes us back Home.

SAFE TRAVELS

We must learn to be the driver of our own life. When we look at people we know, how many are consciously and deliberately creating a wonderful life? Not many. Most are scared, angry, hopelessly-hanging-on, or grin-and-bear-it passengers in the vehicle of their life which seems to be driven by someone other than themselves - God only knows who! Jump in the driver's seat and learn to steer in a confident, calm, and knowledgeable way, and your life will travel along safely and happily.

About the Author

Donna Goddard is an author and shares her love for the Divine and the world with a large international audience. She lives in Melbourne, Australia.

All links https://linktr.ee/donnagoddard

Love and Devotion - next book in series

Love and Devotion is a four-book nonfiction series. To find the great Love, we must, one way or another, die the great death. Once that death is conquered, we won't have to die again. There is a grand and magnificent truth that radiates from within all of life and each of us. May you discover in your heart a sweet lightness, the luminescent glow of God's beauty, and a true appreciation for the wonderful gift of life which glows unmarred through every human error. We are loved by the Divine, loved into existence. That, in itself, is enough to reassure each one of us of our inestimable worth.

- The first book, in the series, is *The Love of Being Loving*. It is about the earlier adult years of my spiritual development. Dr Thomas Hora (Metapsychiatry) and Mary Baker Eddy (Christian Science) were the most significant influences on my spiritual path during my twenties and thirties.
- The second book is *The Love of Devotion.* In my forties, I started reading a series of metaphysical books by Dr David R. Hawkins. I realised that

they were having a potent impact on my growth and Dr Hawkins became my next spiritual teacher. Dr Hawkins (Devotional Nonduality) and Dr Hora came from very similar spiritual and intellectual terrain. We are drawn to a certain field of truth that resonates with our inner leanings. My interest in understanding thought drew me to teachers who also had a deep interest in human consciousness.

- The third book is *Love's Longing*. Somewhere along the way, there develops within the soul a yearning that can no longer be ignored; a craving for the great Love affair.
- The fourth book is *Touched by Love.* It is about our body, relationships, and the spiritual path. It is vital to maintain, understand, and balance each of them. We must strengthen, expand, and extend all the energetic systems of our being. It takes work and commitment, but that is the purpose of life.

Ratings and Reviews

I would be most grateful for any ratings or reviews.

Printed in Great Britain
by Amazon

78694972R00059